W9-AZL-410

WITHDRAWN

Feeling Scared

by Helen Frost

Consulting Editor: Gail Saunders-Smith, Ph.D.

Consultant: Erik Willcutt, Ph.D.
Child Clinical Psychologist
Instructor, University of Denver

Pebble Books

an imprint of Capstone Press

Mankato, Minnesota

Pebble Books are published by Capstone Press
151 Good Counsel Drive, P.O. Box 669, Mankato, Minnesota 56002
www.capstonepress.com

1 2 3 4 5 6 06 05 04 03 02 01

Library of Congress Cataloging-in-Publication Data
Frost, Helen, 1949–
      Feeling scared/by Helen Frost.
      p. cm.—(Emotions)
      Includes bibliographical references and index.
      Summary: A description of fear using simple vocabulary.
      ISBN-13: 978-0-7368-0671-8 (hardcover)
      ISBN-10: 0-7368-0671-7 (hardcover)
      ISBN-13: 978-0-7368-4846-6 (softcover pbk.)
      ISBN-10: 0-7368-4846-0 (softcover pbk.)
      1. Fear in children—Juvenile literature. [1. Fear.] I. Title. II. Emotions
(Mankato, Minn.)
BF723.F4 F76   2001
152.4′6—dc21   00-023054

Note to Parents and Teachers

The Emotions series supports national health education standards
related to interpersonal communication and expression of feelings.
This book describes and illustrates the feeling of being scared. The
photographs support emergent readers in understanding the text.
The repetition of words and phrases helps emergent readers learn
new words. This book also introduces emergent readers to subject-
specific vocabulary words, which are defined in the Words to Know
section. Emergent readers may need assistance to read some words
and to use the Table of Contents, Words to Know, Read More,
Internet Sites, and Index/Word List sections of the book.

Table of Contents

You feel fear
when you are scared.

Fear can warn
you of danger.

8

You sometimes feel scared when there is no danger.

You might feel
scared of the dark.

You might feel
scared of heights.

You can talk
about what scares you.

You can learn more
about what scares you.

You can learn
to be careful.

You can learn
to be brave.

Words to Know

brave—willing to try something that causes fear; being brave can help people overcome their fears.

careful—paying close attention to keep from making mistakes or getting hurt; fear can make people careful.

danger—a situation that is not safe; danger can make people feel scared; people should be careful when there is danger.

Read More

Althea. *Feeling Scared.* Exploring Emotions. Milwaukee: Gareth Stevens, 1998.

Doudna, Kelly. *I Feel Scared.* How Do You Feel? Minneapolis: Abdo Publishing, 1999.

Kreiner, Anna. *Let's Talk about Being Afraid.* The Let's Talk Library. New York: PowerKids Press, 1996.

Leonard, Marcia. *Scared.* How I Feel. Bethany, Mo.: Fitzgerald Books, 1998.

Internet Sites

FactHound offers a safe, fun way to find Internet sites related to this book.

Go to *www.facthound.com*

FactHound will fetch the best sites for you!

Index/Word List

brave, 21
careful, 19
danger, 7, 9
dark, 11
fear, 5, 7

heights, 13
learn, 17, 19, 21
scared, 5, 9, 11, 13
scares, 15, 17
talk, 15

Word Count: 62
Early-Intervention Level: 6

Editorial Credits
Mari C. Schuh, editor; Kia Bielke, designer; Katy Kudela, photo researcher

Photo Credits
Daemmrich/Pictor, 1
David F. Clobes, 6, 8, 10, 16
Frank Siteman/Pictor, cover
Kim Stanton, 14
Matt Swinden, 12
Michael Hart/FPG International LLC, 4
PhotoDisc, Inc., 18
Unicorn Stock Photos/Aneal Vohra, 20

The author thanks the children's section staff at the Allen County Public Library in Fort Wayne, Indiana, for research assistance.